Surfacing

Surfacing

poems

Emily Tuszynska

GRAYSON BOOKS
West Hartford, Connecticut
graysonbooks.com

for my three children, who grew along with this book,
and for my parents

The Neighborhood

We live in green
depths of trees
planted by those
who grew old
and died or moved
away our children
play in yards theirs left
behind and sleep
in rooms that held two
or even three until
they grew our children too
are growing in summer
we box outgrown
clothes repaint
the walls new tiles
for the bath new
shingles the trees
don't seem to change
though of course
they must the backyard
beech and oaks
that will outlast us
casting a deeper
shade the front yard
holly reaching farther
over the drive we pull in
and out of always
in a rush someone
running back for what
they forgot the trees
keep some other kind
of time spend whole

seasons taking in
their sustenance
strange food
without substance
every summer
a feast of light

Contents

At Home

in this small house, made smaller still
by the massive hardwoods overhead,

the children wake us every hour,
first one calling and then another

as the moon floats through the window
like a slow bubble through syrup.

It shrinks as it rises, finally arcing up
and out of the window frame

and releasing the house into shadows
through which we walk in turns as walls

give way and ceilings drift into rustling
leaves. Experience has taught me

a division of the self—one half of the mind
still sleeping while the other wakes

to watch the body carry its mute
comfort like a glass of water

to a child. I think a part of me
will be alive in this night forever—

rolling to meet your returning warmth,
rising to leave you sleeping as I balance

across a cool floor that materializes
and vanishes underfoot. Your song

as you walk the baby is a strand of dream
from which I wake to find myself singing,

holding a child dense and solid
with sleep. Fans drag damp air

in a vaporous river through the rooms.
From the treetops a thousand insects cry,

and the sound sinks straight through me.
Every barrier is lifted, every boundary

broken. Even my heart is unguarded.
Are you still there? a child whispers—

and whose is the voice that answers?

On the Bridge

The boy stopped to push
his sticks through the railing,

solemnly opening
his hands for the pleasure

of feeling them emptied,
then turning to see

the twigs catch
and spin and slip over

the spill between stones.
White sycamore-tops hung

in the boundless sky.
The wind moved there

apart from us,
the branches shook

and released their leaves
as the dead must shed

even their deepest memories.
Summer was gone

but he remembered
the dim green of it.

Time was welling up,
drawing him forward

into its current.
When the bright shapes

came clattering down
through the still air

I reached out
to catch one,

given from the tree,
and he waved it

like a flag,
a celebration,

and that was fall,
he named it, shouting.

Peaches

All afternoon I'd been canning peaches in batches,
a heat and a sweetness filling the low-ceilinged kitchen,
glittering mason jars steaming dry on spread towels,
big pots of water and syrup frothing up and subsiding,
the canner constantly chattering, rattling its jars,
the crate under the window emptying slowly—
Later, I lay under the slow-turning fan, closed my eyes,
and saw peaches, peach pits, and shucked peach skins.
Their flesh was so golden the white walls took on their color.
The skin of my fingers was soft and sticky with juice.
You came to the room and hesitated, hand on the doorframe,
said my name softly, distinctly, to see if I slept.
Each syllable came separately into my consciousness
like the half globe of a late-summer peach, slipped
from a ladle into its jar of thick syrup, settling down
to cup itself around the half that came before.

Descent into the Chamonix Valley

We summited in darkness and at dawn
began the descent, the two of us skidding and sliding,
glare-blinded, snow a slurry of wet pearls,

thin air strafing our throats. Wind snapped
our jackets as clouds parted below us.
The snow smelled of minerals, of stone,

it thinned until we balanced across talus
splotched with lichens in rust and lime,
scree rattling loose in the sun's heat.

A crusty soil appeared, with tiny flowers
in the lee of stones and shrubby plants with a sharp,
resinous scent, then misshapen pines,

branches sprawling south along the ground.
The wind was suddenly buffered, pungent with humus
among alders and mossy, tumbled boulders

along a widening stream. The world was emerging
on all sides, new and immeasurable—
there was a path that became a lane, there was a pasture

with white-faced cows, a woodlot and birds
flocking against a deepening sky. Music floated
across a field and a small boy hurried home.

Our boots struck pavement; there was talk and laughter
and the smell of food. Shopkeepers drew down
their rattling grilles as the high peaks flamed and went out.

We took our place on a crowded bus, stooping
to look up through fogged windows as darkness
consumed the landscape. What seemed to be a swath

of night sky was the mountain's vast black flank,
a remnant of light far overhead where stars began.
Together we rode back to where we'd started,
the immense, invisible landscape rising around us.

Firstborn

How marvelous, the way he looked and looked,
even as the two nurses rolled him under the heat lamp,

wiping away blood and meconium and buttery vernix,
re-clamping the thick, violet umbilical cord, bundling him

into a crinkling diaper with a cutout scoop for the stump—
all the while he seemed to study their blurred motions

against the stark geometry of walls and window and door.
Under the fluorescent glare he winced and squinted,

but still he looked, as if no matter how painful, this
was what he came here to do. When they were done

you eased your splayed hands under his scalloped
shoulder blades, his damp, misshapen head, gathering

his bunched and folded limbs and lifting the slumped
weight of him to your chest to bring him to me.

Outside the world was new again with the snow
that had started falling with the onset of labor.

All night the plows rumbled past, scraping the asphalt
clean. The next day we wrote a name on their forms

and worked his limbs into his fuzzy suit and buckled him
into his seat. At the doors we paused on the brink of a day

turned dazzling. Overnight the fresh snowfall had been split
by seams of salted pavement. We looked at it straight on,

this blinding world, taking its measure, and then together
we carried him into it, full of tenderness and dread.

Nocturne

Everything close and familiar has shifted
slightly. Off kilter. Floor at a slope, walls aslant.
In the darkness the crib is just out of reach and then
there in my hand, rail too high and surprisingly solid.
For so many nights the baby's stammering cry
has uprooted me from sleep that tonight
I woke not for sound but for silence, wet sheets,
and the heavy ache in my breasts. Now I hesitate,
hand on the crib rail, milk dripping,
holding my own breath to hear the sound of his.
Sleep has stolen him from me, me from him;
a river floods the seam newly sprung open
between us, leaves me stranded on the far shore.
The room's unbounded, walls receded to forest,
nowhere a path to lead the way home.

Postpartum

I keep coming back,
keep climbing the stairs
to push the button
that lets the slow notes fall,
keep making my face rise
like the moon over your crib,
keep letting my hand
be the weight to teach
your small body stillness.
Like lilies your fists unfurl.
Dusk obscures the corners
of the room, and the walls
expand, the way each day
since you came
has become an ocean,
the sharp pull of your need
through the shapeless hours
the thing that keeps me
from drowning.

Ceiling

The utter darkness made of that cramped
room a vast space that we spoke into
without turning toward one another,

our words unscrolling above us
invisibly. *It's all right,* you said,
the baby mumbling and moving

against the bars of his port-a-crib
and so you—*I've got him*—your voice
moved away and then returned, softer,

hand whispering along the wall,
to put him down between us
where he lay soothed by our talking,

our voices interlayering in the stale air
with long pauses now as each word,
even the slightest, seemed to condense

into its meaning. Almost palpable,
they left our lips and floated drowsily
to the ceiling, growing richer and darker

with all they contained, taking on a lustrous,
transparent blackness, until at last we fell
into a deep calm, and I dreamt of a roof of words

we dismantled, grateful to be working together
in a cadence not unlike that of speaking,
handing down words and discarding them

in piles here and there as we took them out,
leaving behind gaps that came together
slowly to form the whole sky.

Maternity Leave

My husband brings the baby and a kiss
to where I lie in milk-wet sheets,
ripe as a pomegranate,
slick and sweet.

Hello, little slippery mouth, hello
my blind little fish, right here
my squirming one,
all searching lips and squinched eyes,
limp as soon as he latches,
cheek and eyelid beaded with milk.

Already the air at the screen
is heavy and still, the light tinged
green by new leaves.

Look at me lounging, an odalisque.

At last the baby heaves himself off
the breast with a satisfied smack
and lolls into a milk-drunk stupor.

I hear my husband's car
pull out of the driveway,
and then the neighbor's car,
the one with the noisy muffler,
starts up and drives away.

Everyone's busy but me.

Every Day a River

Once more the day's small boat
carries us downstream,
the baby and I together,
passing the milky backwaters
of sleep, our journey marked
by a series of bundlings
and unbundlings—*There is your hand!*

We drowse between banks
tangled in willow and birdsong,
water tapping from the oars,
only to find ourselves
arrived, barefoot, in the kitchen—
the teakettle's bright whistle,
the cool floor a bewilderment
of sun and shadow.

The same grass still pools
around the house, bright green
where it was dull,
and stippled now with white
and yellow. The baby in my arms
has grown sun-brown
and sturdy—cheeks tight,
bare thighs fat and creased.

A mockingbird taps
and taps at his reflection,
now at the bedroom window,
now the living room,
marking the glass
with a haze of wing prints.

Nobody Told Me

about this intense happiness that comes
squeezed between the fatigue and anxiety
and the endless repetition necessary
to keep a baby alive and mostly not-crying:

an expanding exhilaration that is equal parts
relief at being once more alone in my body
and a sense of rightness at last—
always before too tall and awkward,

flat-chested and unsure what to do
with my hands. Now my narrow hips
have proved their competence, my breasts
have acquired new dimensions.

Yes, death waits—in the promise written
into our wedding vows, in the contract
all parents sign at a child's birth. But my body
knelt and opened, and in the ferocity of that opening

taught me the strength of earth's relentless urge
toward existence, toward the two of us walking together
through today's trumpet blare of spring sun and wind,
toward the boy in my arms, the day's darling,

eyes wide and brows raised under his little cap,
mouthing his fist and pressing his toes
hard against the feet of his sleeper,
kicking his legs for the sheer joy of it.

What Vanishes

Winged brown shapes flicker
in the forsythia hedge, bobbing,

drab flames that gutter amid frail
flower flames. *Birrr,* the child trills,

triumphant at naming what he sees.
The bushes are full of motion,

a constant flitting and resettling
of feathers, blurred flights out and back.

Birr. He thrusts his feet against my hip,
himself bobbing; he reaches as if to seize

the birds mid-flight. The world breaks
into distinctions of *bird* and *flower* and *bush*—

bright words winging into his mind,
bringing each thing up, particular,

out of a disintegrating whole. As we approach
there's a startled up-lifting, glimpsed and gone—

sparrows flushed from the bushes,
flurry of feathers and wing-beaten wind,

appearing and then disappearing
in the moment of appearance.

When the boy was new, and nameless,
we inhabited together an unbroken

shimmering realm, hidden beneath
all that can be articulated.

Now word by word I'm luring him
into this world that scatters before us.

Flowers, Moon

Spring. And the boy is walking, wearing his new
soft-soled shoes, green leather with a black bear
stitched onto the toe. *Shoes,* he said, clear as anything
when I sat him in my lap to put them on.

He doesn't want to be carried, doesn't want
to ride in his stroller. I button his corduroy coat
and tie his hat and we go out under the windy sky.
He sets his feet down hard, feeling the flagstones,

wobbles into a squat beside the crocuses, first flowers
of his second year. Months have passed
with hardly any color, and now the buds unclasp,
six petals making purple stars around six golden anthers.

He touches with one finger, ducks his head to whisper
a syllable I stoop to hear. *Fluh.* Another word
to expand his kingdom. The moon too is cause
for exclamation. We search the sky until he finds it

starting over, slenderest white nick in the blue.
There's so much he doesn't know. Why *not* start
with flowers, with the moon's dependable return?
Nothing stops the world's desire to go on unfolding.

Incarnate

after Desiderio da Settignano's marble tondo "Meeting of Christ and John the Baptist as Youths"

Under Desiderio da Settignano's tools, the two boys must have
pressed up and out as through a veil, a caul, the marble block

warmed by his polishing, as if stone were transmuting to skin,
mouths panting softly, opening, soft eyes opening in luminous

stone. *Open. Open.* That prayer of childbirth, a desperate
willed acceptance, choosing what can't *not* be chosen: the body's

dumb surrender. *Be broken, torn;* be opened, flayed; be naked,
shaking. Desiderio, what tore you open? Though your story's lost,

these your stone children bear the sweet mark of sorrow,
and of the end you knew—John's bearded head on a platter,

the gush of blood and water from Christ's side,
and before the mystery of mysteries, the temple curtain

ripped in two. Oh, flesh. Wail, moan, be touched, be torn,
until we know the body to be nothing more than the wound

through which the spirit is pierced. *Stay, stay,* your chisel rang,
and fell silent. Almost six centuries later these two boys,

cut and hammered into existence, cannot stop themselves,
they must grasp each other. They are, yes, *made flesh.* Their hands

sink into John's fleece tunic and they quiet themselves
to feel the heart repeating its one muffled note of astonishment.

How many times, Desiderio, did you put down your tools to touch
Christ's cheek, here, where generations of living hands have rubbed

the sensuous marble smooth? Did you feel what Mary felt
as she touched Elizabeth—the stirring of a boy within the womb?

Expectant

I.

I'm the wave before
it breaks the ground before
it quakes the maelstrom
before it hits the water
before it boils the word
before it forms.
                My mind
is a blank.
I expect _____.

In truth I don't expect,

I *am*—
       mind gone
deep into my solid heft.
Doubled, divided,
              am I
              not whole
or is it *more so*,
            gasping
up the stairs, heaving
my bulk into bed,
first the torso then
the legs.
         My air—divided.
My blood—divided, my
body—divided, my heart—
my heart.

II.

Not the wave
but what's driven
under, not the storm
but what staggers through,
drenched and searching for you,
like water, you surround me,
I push into
                        the raw scent
of your birth-sac
                        breaking
you're
        here,
                here,
Still you won't . . . no matter how
I position
                myself
                        you
won't show.
                The present
is bearing down
into the future yet again
and I'm the blocked
                        conduit,
because birthing you whole—
crumple-faced newborn,
taut-bellied toddler, adolescent
hair in your face and silence,
and your love, your children,
they're here,
                        and yes
most yes your death,
                it's that death

which I'm
            birthing,
                        working
so hard to expel, fire
that I cannot
                I cannot
let my mind
            float
loose

my beautiful child,
my beautiful
                not-me child
my beautiful mine-to-let-go
child you eviscerate me,
I'm spent, I'm split,
fine spray of blood
the nurse is trying to catch
my eye
            listen she says listen
there's no way but through
and you come
                slick and skidding
I'm broken, I'm two.

Night Waking

He wants to be rocked, walked, soothed:
awake at 1:15, at 2:00, at 3:05, and I can
not hold him any longer—

I find myself driving our mazy streets,
one hand slung behind the headrest
to stroke his cheek, the other palming

the wheel I am too tired to grip.
Only loosely am I connected to my self
which seems to drag far in our wake,

its many desires dwindled to specks
faint as the city stars. Even the craving
for sleep has worn away, leaving resigned

acceptance and a gratitude for night's
emptiness which comes each evening
at the same hour to enfold us.

My dark head facing forward, his downy one
facing back, we're both quiet, calmed.
The car's steel frame sways

above its chassis, almost floating;
I'm loose, sliding on vinyl—no seatbelt
at this slow speed. Stop signs

loom up in reflective radiance and we
drift through, turning at every corner.
Not a lamp in any window,

and only once, far down a straightaway,
does another car cross, trailing its taillights'
vanishing glow. Everything is more beautiful,

more singular, in my fatigue. The parked cars
on either side reflect engine noise
in staticky spurts of sound.

Here and there a porch light flares,
leaves sliding like black lace
across its glow as we pass. Flashes,

glints, and streaks of light: mysterious
gleams move over the parked cars,
over the windows of houses

where my lights must glide
along shadowy bedroom walls,
bend onto ceilings, and fade.

I take turn after turn,
circles within circles at the center
of the sleeping neighborhood.

Ars Poetica with Breast Pump

I stay late at work for time
to write (burnt decaf, slick
keyboard on a formica desk,
locked door, and the clutch/sigh
of a hands-free double electric pump)
a poem about the luminous

happiness that blindsided me in our
firstborn's mid-infancy. His babyhood
is gone now, evaporated with our second
son's arrival. Today I saw him tread
heavily, intentionally, on his brother's
hand, then slink away in guilty
satisfaction as the crying started.

When I get home I'll hold both boys,
read a board book to the older
as the baby roots after the milk
I've just siphoned for tomorrow's sitter.
He'll feed hard, yank at the nipple,
cry to nurse again within the hour.

Meaningmeaningmeaning, the pump sighs.
Isn't that what I've stayed
to search for?— dragging reluctant
words into sentences, turning my back
to the children, to my husband,
who's home in front of the open fridge,
baby in one arm, three-year-old methodically
opening and slamming the cupboard doors.

How does one fully inhabit one's life?
The present shatters, remains stubbornly
out of reach, like the children's faces—
half-formed, they flicker with intimations
of past and future selves that I can't
push through to see them as they *are*.
By what paradox do these words
stacked in precarious columns make their subject
at once both more real and also unreal?

The spurting milk slows and I have to pause
to visualize the baby: his scent, his cry,
his searching mouth with its peaked blister,
his fist twisting my shirt . . . until again the milk
lets down. Ounce by ounce the twin bottles fill
with the thin fluid, its topping of cream.

Saturday

I wheel the weekly route through the produce section's
artificial year-round bounty, up and down the aisles

as the cart slowly fills, baby slung across my chest.
In the checkout I nuzzle his velvet head and breathe

the smell of him, clean sand and salt. The heat of him,
sun-warm under my cheek. The moment ripens

until my throat aches with it, even here in the supermarket,
waiting to pay, waiting to go home, where my husband

cuts decking boards as our four-year-old plays in the late sun.
The saw whines and falls silent, whines and falls silent,

segmenting the afternoon. In between there's the dull clatter
of wood on wood and the braided sound of conversation,

my son's voice lilting over his father's lower responses.
I set the bags on the kitchen floor and nurse the baby,

then brace him on my hip to peel potatoes.
Steam blurs the darkening windows. Nights are not deep

here in the suburbs. Their black no more than gray,
and only a paltry handful of stars. Still, after supper

I bathe the baby and take him in his fuzzy sleep sack out to see
the moon's sliver, the few stars glinting through.

He reaches for them, solemn in the shifting air and light.
And again I can feel the moment grow to its true size,

or I think I can. This moment and the next.
What will stay? When all that is passing

has passed. *I thought I would remember
everything*, J. told me. Meanwhile the baby

will not sleep unless I stand and rock him, repeating
a little square of step and sway in his darkened room.

When I'm out of songs I watch the clock and count
time passing. *Two minutes. Three.* Each day he's heavier

though I cannot feel it, until now he's almost more
than I can bear. Even away from him, at work, I'm bruised

by tenderness. Glint of his eyes in darkness.
Two more minutes. Three. Stoop for the pacifier

off the floor. *Three more. Four.* Little baby boy
come to lodge with us, good night. Keeping the weight

of my hand on him, hunched over the crib.
Two more minutes. Three more. Four. I hold the latch

to close his door without a sound and slip down
to the bright quiet where my husband reads in lamplight,

smelling of sawdust, our older boy long since put to bed,
the counters wiped, still-warm dishes put away.

I drift free of the day on the couch, half-sleeping,
half-listening for the stirring of the baby, who up the stairs

is too far to hear. Instead, there's the sound of a helicopter
beating overhead, on its way to some aftermath. And something

I cannot comprehend. A quiet voice here in this room.
Unintelligible syllable out of the silence. So soft

it's almost in my own mind. Pausing. Repeating. Insistent.
The small word each page whispers as it turns.

Afternoon

From where I lay next to our sleeping
children after nursing the toddler
for what would turn out to be one of the last times

I could just see a sweep of green branches,
trembling. The breeze picked up
and all the leaves turned together

like the notes of a song falling into place
as the refrain returns, this year's one-year-larger tree
erasing the memory of last year's smaller version,

and you came in and looked at me;
I got up and leaned against your familiar body,
pressed my mouth to your narrow lips

that both of our boys have inherited,
and we stood for a moment
as still as our sleeping children

just hearing the four separate sounds
of our breathing. And we were a family,
I felt it there in that small space of rooms

ordinarily so full of our noisy motion, the four of us
crossing paths full tilt, weaving our tangled
trajectories together into our own particular cloth.

The Wind at South Core Bank

Through the noisy inhale of our yearly stay
the cabin waits to exhale into its empty state:

sand-swept floors, silvered salt-damp beadboard,
uncurtained windows open for airing. Wind roars

like an endless rising tide around the corners, sifts sand
against window screens, and entering, stirs the idle fan

into a frenzied swirl. It turns down the children's blankets
and flips wet towels from the line above their bunks.

Restless, it washes through louvered interior walls,
scatters napkins, cards, lifts the tablecloth and lets it fall,

then takes its never-ending leave and slams the door.
Time runs backward for the child standing on the shore,

naked feet braced in a tumbling cosmos of broken shells,
sailing at dizzying speeds against the sucking rush

as I imagined myself sailing backward, a child standing
so long ago on the same shifting, escaping sand—

as we all sail, riding this changing, changeless week of time
like kites, rising on the tension between wind and steadying line.

Tundra Swans at Mason Neck

At any moment half the swans are airborne,
birds loping awkwardly into heavy flight
only to veer back for another splashdown,
their wakes unzipping the sky's half-frozen image.
Over everything floats the constant,
urgent clamor of their multitudinous calling,
layered voices airy with an arctic emptiness
brought to this protected edge of a landscape
rivered by highways, its parking lots
glittering like open water from the air.
Another winter at the refuge,
though projections show their winter territory
leaping north within ten years. There's no
permanence. Just this cacophonous splendor,
the children too now running in circles, flapping
and shouting, birds wheeling and landing and rising,
the winter marsh all wind and current and wing.

The Bone Suit

Beneath his skin's thin cloth
his own bones guide me.
Over a white-sponged base

I smudge two black rectangles,
rounding them up to the brow rim,
out to the eye-socket's arch,

then rub shadow into the temples
and beneath the cheekbones' slope.
Leaning close, I grease-pencil

fractures onto his forehead
and bared teeth over his lips.
When I stand him to the dark

glass of the window, his image
blurs enough to look like
the real thing—gaunt death's grin

on his soft, six-year-old face.
I'm there too, hesitant shade
touching his shoulder. Black deep

in the reflected hollows of our eyes.
Leaves of the backyard holly
stirring in that blackness.

What is this wilderness
we carry? Something more
than death. Of which death

is only a part. His father takes him
into the night, this boy
whose time and space of living

overlap our own. Walking
from one lighted door to another,
bells ringing, voices and footfalls

twining through shadow.
At last they turn toward home,
his bag grown heavy

with sweetness. He sits on the floor
to shuck bright wrappers
and eat, wiping his lips

on his black, boned sleeve,
until from the paint
his own familiar mouth emerges.

Windows at Twilight

Lamps shine out there, knotted in rhododendron.
Rooms emerge, filled with the susurration of leaves.

The leaves fill all the dark spaces—maple in open cabinets
and hickory in the fireplace. Saplings spring up from tile.

This season the forest is dulled by drought. The tree trunks
piercing the ceiling rise like columns of smoke.

Here, in the kitchen's bubble of incandescent light,
the warm dishwater, the sleepy calls of the children,

the grocery list on the counter—milk, bread, fruit—
all of them vouch quietly for the ordinary.

A sudden rush of damp air sends the walls swaying
and a few leaves come down from the highest branches,

but no rain falls. Lightly, lightly, my mind touches what I love.
I'm here, and I'm not here—

I'm the luminous face in the glass, the one who turns aside
past the suspended bowl of pale flowers,

who walks among tulip trees hung with paintings.
Picking things up, putting them down.

How does one know what one is looking for?
A bed of bracken. A stone on which to lay my head.

Enough. Put out the lights, one by one. Extinguish the rooms,
great white flowers closing for the night.

The massive, swaying trees cohere. In their depths,
small creatures go about the seed and crumb business of living.

Only the lamp in the hall still burns.
Beyond, our bed's comfortable disarray.

To move toward it sends my reflection—
bare-headed, empty-handed—into the fern-dark forest.

The Nest

For days it has moved
from one spot to another—
bookcase, table, counter,
bathroom—shedding
stray bits of twig
and flecks of moss.
None of us can keep
from handling it—
testing its springy resilience,
tracing the intricate weave
of root tendril and fiber,
strands of hair
and shreds of grass.
The bottom is worn
almost through.
Only an open, meticulous
meshwork remains.
Woven into this whorled
lace of thread
and hair and stem
is the weather-softened
flag of paper
from a chocolate kiss,
repeating its one word:
DARK   DARK   DARK.
There the eggs must have rested,
warm pearls carried
among drifting branches.
From out of summer's lush heat,
this frail coracle.

Inhabiting the Pregnant Body

The weight I carry
is the weight of the past.
What's buried there
is buried in me. The hand
with which I rub a response
to the baby's kick is not my hand
but the hand of my mother,
and the song I hum
is one my grandmother sang.
What never dies
flows through us
like a river.
Deep in the folds
of my unborn
daughter's body, the future
has already formed.

Floodplain

All morning in mid-labor
not ready for the hospital

        walking the floodplain

     the earth still soft
     waters receded

              tulip poplars
              knotted sycamores
              clumps of grass

ghosted with silt

the trees leaned downstream
from many floods

             I clung to them

my sisters I thought if I thought at all
somehow the term did not seem wrong

the ground was washed bare

          fibrous roots exposed

slack water
dusty with pollen

we walked and rested and walked again

bowing

then kneeling

to each contraction as it came

some bright bit of blue
caught on the far bank

without panic
I felt each crest carry me farther
away from you

away from familiar ground

in the spaces between

your hands

lightly—

the air on my face—

maybe I *was* the trees

their massive trunks shifting
as wind poured
through high branches

perhaps I was the riverbed

or the light as it pulsed between moving leaves

from all about us
a wordless insistence

deep in my interior

the forest   the water rising

In the Milk Bed

I.

Yes, the world made way, opening once more.
What choice does it have but to go on?

The two of us mark a place where time
turned inside out, dropped
through itself,
your head tucked, looking back
into the past.
The old world
you were born out of remains
unredeemed,
irreparable—

Yet here in the house cleaned for your coming,
the antique bed has been made with new sheets,
the doors and windows
have all been opened.

The pliant limbs of the willow oak give way
as if to usher in this breeze that blows, night and day, from the
east.

Summer is fully fledged. It trembles at its own excess.

All morning two falling notes,

then two falling notes.

Little chickadee, high
in the sunlit willow oak at the east window,

then deep in the cypress at the north.

Brief song handed back and forth.

One for sorrow, two for joy, isn't that how it goes?

Joy then, I'll take that,
along with my ice packs,
my cabbage leaves
and compresses. And you
that I can hardly call my—
I'll try—unpacked bundle
I scoop onto my slack stomach.

Your star hands flex and wander
your blurred heaven.

II.

Somewhere far below, the shriek and thump of your brothers
washes in and out of the house like a tide. Below that
the groan of distant traffic, and the soft, strange wind,
and below that . . . an almost imperceptible grinding.
The slow wheel of time consumes the present moment.
and below that, below that . . .

You grope to latch and fail, again, again,
startle yourself
with a thin
strained wail,
gape-mouthed,
my huge hand guiding your head
in to try—*there*—press—

you clamp wide
we teeter
on the brink— kick away a sheet of pain—
and you—and we—are falling, drifting
through the wilderness below thought,
into pure perception.

Shifting branches fill the windows and mirror,
continually swept aside
and then falling back into place.

World veiled, unveiled.

Beguiled, beguiling, and guileless.

The wind is the world's emissary,
and we open our doors and windows to it.

III.

Everything seems impossibly distant
and also unbearably close.
I'm weeping again
for the children's
days-long dying. Ambulances
waiting at the blockade.
The mind continually
scraped raw.
Today they write
still searching the Atlantic
for bodies.

Likely never recovered they write.
       The 1, the 12, the 82, the 126
       let fall.
A flash in the sky and a rapid vertical descent.

              Daughter, your fire is laid in ashes.

One room among rooms
beyond number,
east window carried up at last into morning sun.
The beveled edge of the mirror
flicks its light into the swept corners.

       Everything intermingles.
            The pain at the breast
indistinguishable from the sweet
         ache in the palms
          as the milk lets down,
and the blood, the afterpangs.

       I can't tell the difference between joy and despair
           and something deeper still.

IV.

Slowly, now, distinctly. In the foreground of hearing:

Two notes,

                 two notes.

Where is this spring's moss-flecked nest
with its six speckled eggs? The boys and I
searched but couldn't find it.
Maybe the black snake already knows.

One thing,
          and then one thing,

and then another.

The bedside petals edged in fuchsia,

and then their fragrance, come round again

and reaped for joy.

Surely goodness, surely mercy . . .

Everywhere one turns, abundance.

First Breath with Thistledown

Hot, but with a breeze,
       and the breeze carries something
              faintly seen. Small glistenings

against the pines. It is the day's
       zenith, and the summer's.
              A goldfinch sways on a thistle

in a fold of field.
       She sows the slow
              currents of air and the seed

floats down to where we are.
       Our last child has been set
              loose from me. She drifts,

content in her swinging seat,
       her hands rowing through
              shadow. Just weeks ago

she arrived—borne along
       like all of us, sailing
              her little craft of breath

and bone into this restless,
       airy realm. Her first night
              I listened as she learned

to breathe, unsteady
       rhythm of inhale
              and exhale interspersed

with squeaks and snuffles,
        her palm's-width chest
                first pistoning, then barely

stirring under my light hand.
        One moment she is a solid,
                fierce mass, radiant

with her own, internal heat,
        and the next she is light
                as air, asleep

in a loose curl on my chest,
        rising and falling
                on each breath.

Floating, turning, gone.
        Thistledown quivers
                over the gully, falters

over Queen Anne's lace.
        Rising, it disappears against
                the bright sky and then

reappears, eddying at the far side
        of the field. Far, farther—
                almost too far to be seen.

At the Solstice

Blanketed in breath and air,
the children sleep, still points
in their stirring room.

Fans click and hum, and papers,
pages, scotch-taped paintings
rise and fall, waving
a languid good night
and good night and good night.

Curtains swell,
the mobile spins, the bright fish
swims around his wire.

The long evening's light flows in
like water. The mirror receives it,
glass brimful, and pours it out again.

Raspberries

in memory of Marek Tuszynski (1939-2023)

Marek picks raspberries one-handed for his granddaughter,
who rides his hip and watches, mouth opening
at his hand's approach. The berries are faintly fuzzed,
so ripe they're almost purple. *Maliny,* he says.

Kochana. Words in a language she'll never know.
To ease her teething he lets her gum the stub of his index finger,
squared off at the last knuckle. His own wartime childhood
was full of walking, his father escaping the camps,

walking back to Warsaw, the family walking, looking for safety,
looking for work, for food, for a roof that didn't leak,
for spring air that didn't smell of decay,
his mother taking the children to look for their father,

separated again for a reason he doesn't remember,
or maybe never knew. Because of the war, that's all.
He was young; he doesn't remember the villages
where they stayed, where they slept, what they ate,

how many miles they walked, taking turns with the baby.
He remembers sunshine, a game of pulling a clattering scrap
of tin on a string over pavement; he remembers soldiers
who came to a door at night only to beg for potatoes.

He remembers corpses among brambles, remembers a garden
where his father worked for a season. High in a tree
hung a single untouchable peach; he remembers his longing.
One by one he presses berries into his granddaughter's mouth.

She gives her whole self to the eating, the tasting.
With each berry, she turns deeply inward, as if lost in reverie,
though for her I think the past has not yet begun, and the future
is only the next berry, the one she sees in her grandfather's hand.

Night Train

The interior landscape shifts, erodes.
    While the children sleep we shore it up
        with flotsam but the next day another

tide-bitten chunk of coastline
    crumbles. The trouble is we're living
        all at once. We keep rearranging the rooms

to find a way to fit. By day we push
    aside the clutter, lay the baby
        on the floor she drums with open palms

as if to feel it's there. Something solid
    underneath. Mostly everything sways.
        A tree falls and the house next door

stands empty for years. The boy holds his sister
    to the window and shows her how
        to wave goodbye, and that's the morning,

fingerprints in the dust of it. The day moves away
    in all directions. On leafless winter nights we hear
        a train we've never seen on its way to some unknown

destination. If we were on it, I'd lean my head against
    the window's rattling, icy glass, look through our reflection
        at the moon rushing through branches.

Look, there's a farmhouse, miles from the lights
    of any town. Someone turns on a lamp in a window;
        someone stands there, watching us go past.

The Tether

I.

Again and again
the path

turns aside, fretting its way
downslope—

foot-slicked, unscrolling.

On all sides, the blurred,
shifting forest,

expansive architecture
of its canopy

grown up from
the untended,

the wounded ground.

Multiflora rose
snags out into the path.

How does one live
with one's whole heart?

How to wrench open
the last chamber

of that fisted, clenching
creature, the heart

snared in the corporeal,
in sinew and bone.

Always something
held in check.

Something that watches:

the fox, hanging back
in the brambles,

the deer, motionless,
then erupting

away into the rank growth
of the floodplain.

II.

The layered
cathedral ceiling shudders

over the beaten path.

Everyone I care for
lies sleeping

and I'm out here
pounding

my feet
against the hill

as if the day itself

will part before me
and grant entry

into its deepest being.

Each dawn
I lace my shoes

in a small gesture
of departure.

Head down,
breathing hard,

waiting
for downhill's

loose-limbed release,

the burrowing descent
into sycamore and maple.

The path is my light
tether, a cord

that swings me
back to my starting place.

III.

Mid-February,
and the slim buds of the beeches

are still firm.

Not yet the great stirring,
not yet

the unstoppable unfurling,
the softening,

the unshackling.

Just the tightly
rolled rhododendron leaves,

the waxy, spiked hollies.

I run into my solitude,
stiff and slow,

leave no tracks
on frozen ground.

Maybe I am
my own shadow,

tagging along
just behind the present moment.

Reluctant guest,

Whatever
I have been offered,

I have taken
only a portion.

Whatever I have given,
I have held back more.

Not so the Japanese wisteria,
brazen invader,

pushing into sunlight.

Its dry vines leap
into treetops,

weave an opportunistic
smothering crown

for this ragtag
woodland,

this derelict ground.

Even before the vines' leaves
expand, their clustered flower buds

will swell and open,

the path below
will be littered with petals.

IV.

A last upslope
through the forest's edge

choked in honeysuckle,

then the jolting step
onto sun-warmed asphalt.

Houses
line the sidewalk,

each in its own
patch of lawn.

Mine is the third
from the end,

the one with grass
rubbed away beneath the swing.

Here's my cracked,
concrete walk,

my stunted dogwood,

my wrought-iron railing—
and here's my life,

the one I chose.

It slides along
behind the door,

in the voices
of my children,

awake and quarreling,

in the clink of dishes
against a glass tabletop.

Here's my hand
on the worn knob,

and here I am,
pushing open the door,

here I am,
entering.

Returning Home in Midwinter

Like a boat sliding onto shore, the car bumped into the gravel drive,
rattling my sleeping head against the window. For a long time

the moon had swung its lantern this way and that, and now
in its light our house stood, both familiar and utterly strange—

its windows black, its porch white with untracked snow.
There was a moment's stillness, and then a jostling

as my parents, so young then, stooped into the backseat's warmth,
half-bundled us into coats, and guided us over snow that creaked

and popped in the midnight cold. The light of the stars
that had wheeled and flocked in our wake touched down

onto an earth shrunken as hard as a peach's bitter almond pit.
That was the year I had begun to grasp the bleak distances

traversed by starlight, an emptiness that had so far been hidden
by my parents' buffering love, which though it could transcend

nothing, still persisted, unremarkable. Love was a sort of current
I swam in: my mother fitting the small silver key into the lock,

my father hoisting me, cupping his hand to the back of my head,
just as tonight we carry our own children over snow, quickly

through the cold, breathing the wheat-salt smell of their hair,
pulled forward by their weight in our arms. I'm burdened,

staggering, the boy I'm carrying is limp with sleep. And love
is not a current but a torrent, a flood I'm wading through.

The house has grown cold in our absence, and the children
huddle into chill sheets, burrowing back into sleep,

leaving us behind as they are carried into their separate worlds.
I go down, turn up the furnace, look out at a night turned curiously

bright—ground white with snow, sky white with cloud,
light reflecting, echoing between the two. Not desire, this love.

A sort of radiating out, an expansion, a dispersal, of the self.
The profligate earth spins it off like the particles of lamplight

scattering now into the dark between stars. The two of us inside,
frost softening on the windowpanes. Though love is inadequate.

Though it drags us under. Making myself busy now with the kettle,
yet listening for the children to wake, to call, to need us to come.

How I Became a Mother

The children were a wilderness
in which I wandered; they were a bend
in the road, a map on which the place names

had been altered. They were a dream
I half-remembered as I dreamed it, a language
I'd never spoken, a taste I hadn't known

I craved. They were a wound that would
not close, and they were the salve
for healing. The children were animals,

and in the forest through which they led me
I was one too; with their small hands
they gentled me. The children were bridle, harness;

they were the weight I carried, the stones
I would never take from my pockets.
They were my snug, my perfect fit.

They were a charm, a chant, a spell that brings
a change of season. They were an opening
through which I plunged, the water

that closed over me; they were a flood, a torrent;
they turned me inside out, and when
I no longer knew myself, they knew me,

they made me flesh, they claimed me.

Inheritance

To ease my daughter into sleep I trace fields
across her back and till the earth with my fingers,

plowing, discing, and harrowing, sowing seed,
back and forth, back and forth, last remnant

of my grandfather's Minnesota family farm,
sold at auction before she or I was born.

I make the good rain fall again, and spread
sun's warmth with open palm across the memory

of land that answered our immigrant ancestors' longing
for wind-swept northern plains and fertile ground.

At last the harvester crawls heavily down
the length of her back, and all that remains is stubble.

Sleep comes to cover her then like a drift of snow.
What place will she find to call her own,

this child of stilt grass and knotweed, of autumn olive's
silver tangle, of the raw force that propels

their ragged stems up from any empty ground?
She rooted herself in me, this child of a country

that leaves its past behind. When she was born
I kissed her every inch as if to make her mine.

The Unmown Field

Ten years gone and even I
who watched every season
of its changing can no longer
remember the field
that's grown over.
Sheltered by snow-toppled
grasses, the green shoots
of trees hardened,
and by the first June
red cedars tongued
the air above bluestem.
Nothing lasts. Not the field,
not my girlhood, not the baby
I carried until the next came
behind him. Now my daughter
is the one who is young,
and already too heavy
to carry. Doves croon
to her from new pines
as they did from the pines
of my childhood. The sorrow
in their song is the sorrow
of the human listener,
old sorrow that somehow
I knew even then.

Beach Pea

Unsheltered, the beach pea blues its glaucous green
against the sun. Between clasped leaves it holds
its own bud and tendril, the way my daughter
hides a secret in her two hands. Likely some stone
or shell. The game is in my not knowing.
I pay half attention, make wild, improbable guesses.
An albatross's egg. A blue whale's tear.

The beach pea doesn't know
where it should grow. The right place conjures it:
a lucky, lonely tousle that roots where nothing's rooted,
where weather changes on a whim.
It flies its bright banner in the storm line,
guards its pollen against scattering wind,
petals closed like a mouth that refuses to answer.
My daughter unfolds her fingers to show me
nothing. An invisible, imagined something
she lets the breeze nuzzle from her palm
the way a horse lips sugar from an open hand.

About her world, the coming one, no one knows.
The beach pea swivels, scribes a shift of wind
across blown sand. For ten thousand years it's made
a kind of certainty from the random circumstance
of storm and drift, the rasp of wave and sand
that opens the seed the sea returns to land.

On the Island

It was the season for wild strawberries
    and we knelt on open ground,
working our fingers down

into the tangle of leaf and stem,
    warp and weft of grass and flesh,
weaving ourselves into the day.

Though a chill came faintly off the water,
    each berry was warm from the sun,
like a tiny ember, or the cleansing coal

the angel pressed to the prophet's tongue.
    All afternoon in the company
of those I loved, I held sweetness

in my mouth. Gradually we spread
    across the hillside, wind washing
through the spaces between us.

Now and then we called out
    to one another, our voices rising
effortlessly over the field.

Ordinary words. Words I have long since
    forgotten—soft sounds carried
back and forth, circled by the island's shore.

The Way It Began

At the end of the day's walking there was a ghost town,
though there was nothing left really, just a strange

geometry to the forest. Soil had laid itself down over everything
but each tree with its spare garland of leaves

was a breath, a bright ghost, hovering. The grass was vibrating
in the wind coursing down from the ridge, the light

was humming with what went out from that place.
An invisible engine seemed to churn the air between us.

Everything was in motion there—spangled, dancing—
a low thrumming I could feel in the ground . . .

I reached for you then—didn't I? Wasn't that the way it began?

Child at Pier Cove

Each time you surface it is the same—a widening circle
you swim toward and penetrate, and again the cove

springs into being—the same, and yet subtly changed,
wind off the water increasingly raw, the smallest noises

grown somehow more distinct. Under the unsteady surface
you move as effortlessly as thought untethered

by the advent of sleep, the blank, muffling engine-noise
of a far ship throbbing across distance to surround you.

Then the surface-line touches your forehead, eyelids,
lips—The world returns, at once immediate

and remote, the other swimmers all gone in, the icy creek
cutting across an almost empty beach. With each resurfacing,

the scene takes on a greater depth: a sense of distance
beyond the trees, a certain fullness pressing from underneath,

ripening the dunes. The adults are taking down the umbrellas,
folding the towels. Soon your mother will call you to shore.

Water shifts up and down the pilings, concealing,
revealing. Yes, the darkening trees are a mystery,

and the evening breeze a spirit, moving restlessly
over the face of the water. The sound of the water

is the sound of its name, a whispering that can never
be stilled, though the mind may grow numb to its hearing.

Afternoon Sun at the End of Summer

The children wade naked and thigh-deep
in stone-colored water. They duck under
and come up flinging drops from their hair.
Wind raises gooseflesh on their arms.
Touch is the miracle, wrote Whitman.
Touch is the earth's language and the children
speak it. They revel in it. Wind and water,
and the hard, wave-patterned sand underfoot.
Sound, in its flutter against the inner ear,
and light's weightless impingement
on the seven receptive layers of the retina.

About the Author

Emily Tuszynska lives with her family in Fairfax, Virginia, just outside Washington, DC. Her poetry has appeared in journals such as *EcoTheo Review*, *Mom Egg Review*, *Poetry Northwest*, and *The Southern Review*, and she is the recipient of several awards and fellowships. *Surfacing* is her first collection of poetry.

Acknowledgments

Grateful acknowledgment is made to the editors of the publications in which many of these poems, some in alternate versions, first appeared: *Atlanta Review, Calyx, Crab Orchard Review, The Georgia Review, Indiana Review, Ligeia, Literary Mama, Mantis, Mom Egg Review, Mothers Always Write, Mudfish, New Ohio Review, Poet Lore, Prairie Schooner, PRISM International, Rhino, Salamander, Southern Poetry Review, The Southern Review, Sou'Wester, Stirring: A Literary Collection, Summerset Review, Terrain.org, Third Wednesday, Turtle Island Quarterly,* and *Water~Stone Review.*

The poem "Floodplain" also appeared in the anthology *Tree Lines*, edited by Jennifer Barber, Jessica Greenbaum, and Fred Marchant and published by Grayson Books in 2022. The poem "Windows at Twilight" is for Charles Ritchie.

Thanks also to the Virginia Center for the Creative Arts, the Vermont Studio Center, the Mineral School (and the Sustainable Arts Fund), the Sewanee Writer's Conference, the Eastern Frontier Education Foundation, and the Friends of Porcupine Mountains Wilderness State Park for fellowships and residencies that provided the time and space in which to work on these poems. This book would not exist without those who cared for the children or provided their generous feedback or encouragement for the poems. Heartfelt gratitude to you all.